The

Devil-ution of

Society

From a Civilization of Life
to a Culture of Death
to an Age of Insanity

Paul Murano

En Route Books and Media, LLC
Saint Louis, MO

⊕ENROUTE
Make the time

En Route Books and Media, LLC

5705 Rhodes Avenue

St. Louis, MO 63109

Contact us at **contact@enroutebooksandmedia.com**

Cover Credit: Sebastian Mahfood

ISBN-13: 979-8-88870-107-2

Library of Congress Control Number: 2023951630

Table of Contents

Table of Contents

Introduction

When I wrote the first section of this book back in 1999, I was excited to share it with friends and co-workers. It reflected a common-sense Catholic understanding of how the world had radically unfolded morally before the eyes of someone who grew up in the latter part of the twentieth century. Even though the culture had already been deeply conditioned by Hollywood, higher education, and mass media at the time, I thought once people of goodwill read this candid dialogue between two Catholic friends their eyes would be opened, and they'd want to shout these truths from the rooftops with full force to stop the rapid devolution (or should I say, *devil-ution*) in its tracks. Not so.

I was working as a director of religious education at the time and decided to give a copy of the dialogue to a couple of dedicated Catholic women who had been working for me as catechetical assistants. Up to then, they had been very friendly and talkative to me. After I shared the dialogue, I didn't hear from them much, and when I did they mentioned nothing about it. They didn't even offer any polite pleasantries. A year later, I was working at another parish in a similar position. Thinking my last experience might have been a fluke, I gave a copy of the dialogue to three more people who worked for me at the time. They also were devoted Catholics, diligent in their good work for the Church. Nonetheless, their response was similar to that of the previous two ladies: silence. This time I inquired as to their thoughts. I remember getting an ambiguous runaround response that pretty much said nothing. Sadly, the reactions conformed to the *modus operandi* at the time to avoid all talk of Church doctrine on morality, especially sexual morality, as countless souls were being devoured.

With that discouragement, I put the potential manuscript away somewhere and eventually forgot about it. I figured people just weren't ready to confront the cause of our post-Christian society and the deep-seated lies that had already morally deformed two generations of Americans.

Twenty-two years later, my now-wife found the dialogue manuscript buried in a plastic storage bin out of sight and out of mind. In fact, I had completely forgotten about it. To make a long story short, with much exuberance she encouraged me to complete it and get it published. Since we were now well into the 21st century, I added the second part, which includes more recent social and moral movements and events, up to the present time.

The dialogue format makes this book an easy read. The only thing that may make it a difficult read is a hardened heart. That's because hardened hearts close minds. If people are able to let their defenses down and realize the possibility that our moral formation may have been influenced by one lie after another – and that the resulting ignorance may not have been our fault – they can allow this simple dialogue between two friends to change their lives. The demonic forces of contemporary culture may have robbed us of happiness in the past, but they don't have to control our future, or our children's future. In this dialogue, Danny and Joe uncover the lies that lead to death and the truths that lead to life. Their being "out of touch" enables us to recognize how truly out of touch we have become. If we allow God in to heal us, the inspiration from this simple dialogue can be the beginning of a new sense of hope and purpose.

Lastly, although the interlocutors are Catholic, much of the wisdom and insight discussed here can be appreciated by anyone of good will who's willing to follow reason to wherever it leads. Yet, as we allow its futuristic flavor to entice us, keep in mind we take literary license in this endeavor: neither the author nor the Church supports the use of cryogenics on human beings.

It's now time for me to step aside and allow them to talk. Let's eavesdrop on their fascinating conversation and allow it to speak to our consciences and convict our hearts.

Part 1

1965 Meets 1999

From a Civilization of Life to a Culture of Death

Chapter 1

Welcome back, friend!

At a local restaurant/pub ...

Joe: Hello there. Excuse me. I overheard you talking about your family. Are you any relation to Danny MacInnis?

Danny: Ah, yes. Can I help you?

Joe: You're his son? I've got to tell you, you're the spitting image of your father. You even sound like him. He was a good man and a very good friend of mine.

Danny: My father?

Joe: Your father Danny and I go back a long way. You're his junior I assume, since you look and sound just like him. It's rather uncanny.

Danny: Joe? Joe.... is that you?

Joe: Yes, that's my name. How did you know? Your father mentioned me? I'm sorry about what happened to him. Such a tragedy. It's funny, though, he never told me he had a son.

Danny: Joe .. Unbelievable! Joe....it *is* you, isn't it?!

Joe: Son, I'm not sure you know who you're talking to.

Danny: Joe, it's me, your buddy Danny! I'm not my son, I'm me! How have you been!?

Joe: Hey, I don't have time for strange attempts at humor now. Danny and I grew up together. Tell your mother I said hello. I haven't seen her in.. oh.. almost 35 years.

Danny: You mean Donna. Donna's not my mother, Joe. She's my girlfriend. At least she was. And I'm your old friend Danny! Can't you recognize me?

Joe: I'm sorry, I don't have time for this. Have a good day.

Danny: Wait! Look, I'll prove it. The secret you told me the other day about you planning to go to the Beatles concert at Shea Stadium in spite of your parents' wishes. They think the boys from Liverpool are bad influences.

Joe: What! That was over 30 years ago. I think I remember saying that. I ended up going.

Danny: And how about the Yankees game we went to last month? Mickey Mantle hit two home runs – one in the 9th – to beat the Washington Senators.

Joe: Mickey Mantle is dead, and so are the Washington Senators. They're now the Texas Rangers. That game I went to with Danny was back in 1965. Boy, your father must have really filled you in on his younger days.

Danny: Look, I'm not my son, I'm me! You voted for Johnson over Goldwater in the presidential election last year because you want Kennedy's legacy to continue. You also think Goldwater might get us heavily involved with Vietnam. How would I know this if I wasn't Danny!?

Joe: That was the 1964 election, 35 years ago! How in the world do you know this?

Danny: Your sister is thinking of marrying that beatnik guy your parents hate. Your brother got accepted to Yale but turned it down last month to join a commune. You think Robert Kennedy is going to be a better president than his brother John someday. On that one, I agree with you.

Joe: This is weird. *Very* weird!

Danny: Joe, this is Danny. Sit down, let me explain things. This is going to sound crazy to you, I know, but please listen with an open mind. I need you to believe me because I need your help. Your '35 years ago' is my last week. You see, 1965 seems to me like this year, but to you it's the distant past. No, I'm not crazy. In 1965, I went to serve in Vietnam, as you know. But instead of serving out my entire term, I made a secret deal with the U.S. Government. I volunteered for a top-secret government experiment.

Joe: Huh?

Danny: I was so desperate to get out of 'Nam that I signed up to be a human guinea pig. Unknown to the public, medical science at that time was secretly in possession of a way to freeze individuals alive to slow their vital signs to a virtual stop. Ever hear of cryonics? They needed someone at that time to volunteer to be frozen for several decades in order to calculate the results. It was a frightening prospect, but I was desperate. I'm just not cut out for war. These government scientists wanted to discover what cryonics would do to a living human body in order to use it for future endeavors, such as long-term space travel and freezing people before death to garner for them future medical cures.

Joe: This is insane. I think I need another drink. I'm actually starting to believe you.

Danny: They had me sign a contract to pay me big money if I survived. I didn't think I would make it alive over there in Vietnam, so I accepted. Well, long-story short, I was awakened a week ago. They kept

me for observation and let me go – into a world I now
know very little about. To me, it's September 1965.

Joe: But it isn't.

Danny: I'm trying to get used to that. When I woke
up last week it felt like just a night's sleep had gone
by. Eventually, I realized 34 years had passed! So, to
me it feels like the summer of 1965, but to you it's ....

Joe: It's 1999, Danny! 1999!

Danny: That's why I look so young to you. I'm still
25 biologically. Evidently, the experiment was successful. I feel great, but I'm pretty confused, as you
can imagine. With what seemed like one good night's
sleep, I lost 34 years!

Joe: Wow, science fiction has become a reality. This
reminds me a little of *Planet of the Apes*.

Danny: Planet of the *what*?

Joe: Oh, never mind. It was a movie that came out in

1969 – which I guess was your future. I can't believe I'm saying this. This is crazy! Does anyone else know?

Danny: Not yet. The new people in government requested I keep quiet on this.

Joe: Let me ask you one more question so that I can be sure this bizarre story of yours is true. What was the name of the professor in the one class we had together in college back in the spring semester of 1962?

Danny: Dr. Burnam. Intro to Philosophy. You were a business major; I was a philosophy major. You wanted to make money, and I wanted to discover truth. We would always debate the importance of being vs. doing. His class was a catalyst for our doing this. And you had a thing for the young woman sitting directly in front of us.

Joe: Danny, it's you! You're not dead! In fact, it looks like I'm a lot closer to death than you are!

Danny: I knew you'd come around! I didn't think my

best friend would fail to recognize me. There's a lot of catching up I've got to do, Joe. Could you help me? Everyone else will surely think I'm insane.

Joe: We may both be insane, but your memories are too spot-on to be lies. Besides, I can tell now it's you. You haven't changed a bit.

Danny: Literally! For me, it's only been a couple weeks since I've seen you.

Joe: This is amazing. Everyone, including your family, believes you to be long dead! You were officially pronounced MIA in Vietnam back in 1967 after being missing for a while. No one in government has debriefed you? (To the waiter) We'll have a couple of the house beers, please.

Danny: I've been debriefed, but very little. And much of what they said I couldn't understand. I was really eager to get out of government custody and check things out myself.

Joe: So then…. where in the world do I start?

Danny: Anywhere from 1965. It'll all be new to me. All I know is that in my mind Lyndon Johnson is president, the Beatles just invaded America, and most homes now have black and white television sets. *I Love Lucy* and *Leave It to Beaver* are hit shows and swallowing goldfish is the newest rage on college campuses.

Joe: Wow.... I tell you what; you ask questions and I'll do my best to answer. Believe me, a whole lot has happened.

Danny: Well ... did we ever get heavily involved in Vietnam after I left; and are we out of there now?

Joe: Yes on both counts. We've been out for 25 years.

Danny: Who won?

Joe: Well, I guess they did ... and then we did. But nobody really did.

Danny: Did you ever have to use any of those bomb shelters they built? Was there ever that big nuclear war with the Soviet Union everyone was so fearful of? From the looks of things, it seems we may have avoided it.

Joe: It never happened. Not yet anyway.

Danny: But the Soviet Union, what about the spread of Communism around the world? Are we Communist?

Joe: No. The Soviet Union is now dismantled, and Communism is no longer a serious threat.

Danny: Wow! How did that happen? There must have been a whole lot of casualties to alter the stand-off between the West and those countries behind the Iron Curtain!

Joe: Actually, no. Not a single drop of blood was shed. The Soviet Union broke up from within 73 years after it began. No war, no violence.

Danny: Amazing!

Joe: It was topped off with the dismantling of Lenin's statue by the people on Christmas day.

Danny: On Christmas? What a birthday gift to Jesus!

Joe: It was pretty amazing. The people themselves within the Soviet bloc demanded freedom and radical change.

Danny: That's an absolute miracle! Did the pope ever consecrate Russia to Mary's immaculate heart for its conversion, as she requested at Fatima?

Joe: Huh, you remember that. Yes, I believe he did, sometime in the mid-80s.

Danny: The 1980s? Well then, when did the Soviet Union and her satellite nations fall without any bloodshed?

Joe: They began crumbling in the late 80s, not too long afterwards. The fall of the Berlin Wall came swiftly and without violence.

Danny: Wow! I guess the consecration worked, huh?

Joe: Hey, good point. I never made that connection.

Danny: So, whatever happened to Bobby Kennedy? He must have become president by now.

Joe: No, I'm sorry to say he is no longer with us. He was shot down while campaigning.

Danny: No, Joe, I said Bobby Kennedy, not John.

Joe: I know. Bobby was also killed—in 1968 by a deranged gunman in California while running for president.

Danny: What!? You can't be serious! Two Kennedy brothers assassinated!?

Joe: Yes, it was tragic.

Danny: Boy, another great loss for the Kennedy family and the nation. I bet among those most devastated was that civil rights dynamo Martin Luther King. I bet he really mourned Bobby's loss. Robert Kennedy was becoming a champion of civil rights when I left.

Joe: No… that wasn't possible. Martin Luther King had left us the year before.

Danny: Was he exiled for his civil rights advocacy? I knew that would happen! He caused too much of a stir for the political establishment here.

Joe: No, he wasn't deported. Sadly, Martin Luther King also died from an assassin's bullet. It was a decade of political violence.

Danny: Oh no. The 80s?

Joe: No, the 60s. Not too long after you left.

Danny: Amazing. And what's more amazing to me is that there has been so much violence here, but the Soviet Union crumbled without any. Very strange. How did our nation handle these assassinations?

Joe: With lots of mourning and prayer.

Chapter 2

Cultural change

Danny: Hey, Joe, one thing I noticed on my way up here is that black people weren't sitting in the back of the bus and seemed to be relating to white people casually in public. Is this normal now?

Joe: Yes, it is, Danny. Black people have become more fully integrated into society.

Danny: That's good. I actually saw a black guy anchoring the news on TV this week. That's pretty amazing. And women, too. There were actually women anchoring the nightly news. This isn't considered strange anymore?

Joe: It may seem strange to you Danny, but today you'll find around 50% of all news anchors are women. And it's not only news anchors. Women are now in business, government, universities, hospitals, and elsewhere.

Danny: Hospitals? Has there been an increase in nurses as of late?

Joe: I don't think so. I meant women are doctors now.

Danny: Doctors? Women doctors? It'll be a while before I can get used to that. I mean, I know women make great nurses. But doctors now, too?

Joe: And lawyers…. and even senators.

Danny: Fascinating. The next thing you'll tell me is that a black man and a woman have run for president. That would really be something.

Joe: It's happened, Danny. Jesse Jackson ran for the Democratic nomination in 1988, and Elizabeth Dole is running next year for the Republican.

Danny: Jackson? You mean the kid with the speech impediment who used to follow Martin Luther King?

Joe: Yup.

Danny: And Dole. I know that name somewhere.

Joe: Her husband was in the senate and came real close to becoming vice-president in the 1970s. He ran in '76 with Ford.

Danny: I think you mean he *drove* a '76 Ford, Joe.

Joe: No, I meant…. Ah, never mind.

Danny: Hey, to change the subject, I noticed that all televisions are now in color. That's pretty cool. What's that thing you put tape cartridges in? Those rectangular things are tapes, aren't they?

Joe: Yes, I think you mean VCRs. It means video cassette recorder.

Danny: Interesting. And there are so many TV channels now. For us there were only three: NBC, ABC, and CBS. Remember? Now there are almost 100. And another thing I've noticed ... Where are all the cords? It's amazing how many things run without power cords today. I see telephones no longer have them, televisions have cordless remote controls, and record players… well, I guess there may not be records anymore.

Joe: True. Most people have CDs or cassette tapes. And the cordless remotes do seem miraculous at first glance. But we're just so used to them now. You can get all of these contraptions now by just going to the mall.

Danny: Going to what *all*?

Joe: Huh?

Danny: You said you can get these things by going to *them all*. Who all or what all are you talking about? I'd like to check out these modem gadgets, but I don't know who *them all* are. Please enlighten me.

Joe: What? Oh! I didn't say *them all*, I said *the mall*. Malls are groups of stores that are all together in one place. It's pretty convenient for the shopper. I think they began sprouting up in the 1970s.

Danny: Interesting. Don't they fear each other as competition?

Joe: No. It seems to work out for the good of all the stores. But you don't even have to leave the house anymore. Now you can go onto the world wide web.

Danny: I know you can't be talking about the makings of a gigantic spider.

Joe: Ha! You can find a lot of information now just by surfing the net.

Danny: Surfing? I've water skied before, but I've never tried surfing. Besides, what does surfing have to do with finding things ... other than sharks, perhaps?

Joe: Oh no, I'm talking about home computers and the internet. I should have clarified that.

Danny: Whoa, one thing at a time. Do you have robots in the home now?

Joe: Not exactly. But if you had remained asleep a couple decades longer we might have been talking about that, too.

Danny: Speaking of futuristic possibilities, I thought I saw someone talking on the telephone – inside a car! Wow. With all these innovations, I bet we'll probably be putting a man on the moon pretty soon, like President Kennedy had wanted.

Joe: You missed it, Danny. It's happened.

Danny: We did it? Really! That's great! Hey, to shift gears, what ever happened to the Beatles? Are they still the biggest thing since sliced bread?

Joe: They broke up in 1970. It was too bad. Their genre of music was replaced by heavy metal, and then disco.

Danny: It was? How did heavy slabs of metal replace Beatles' music? I don't understand?

Joe: Then came disco, pop, and rap. And we can't

forget Madonna.

Danny: Of course, we should never forget our Blessed Mother, but what is this thing about metal? Was it a fad?

Joe: Huh?

Danny: Pop? Rap? Heavy metal? It sounds pretty violent.

Joe: Now, you're confusing me. Let's just say popular music has changed a lot since the Beatles broke up.

Danny: Well, maybe they'll get back together.

Joe: I don't think so, Danny. John Lennon is gone.

Danny: Maybe he'll come back.

Joe: No, I mean he's dead.

Danny: Dead? How tragic! He's so young. How long was he sick?

Joe: He wasn't sick. He was shot and killed.

Danny: What!? Wait a minute! Let me get this straight. Since I've been out of commission, not only John F. Kennedy, but also Martin Luther King, Robert Kennedy, and now John Lennon – all shot dead? Has this country gone mad?!

Joe: It does seem like it, doesn't it?

Danny: Boy! No other president has been assassinated….. have they?

Joe: Nope. Ronald Reagan was shot in 1981. But he survived.

Danny: Joe, I said president, not actor.

Joe: Ronald Reagan was president – after being an actor.

Danny: You're kidding. An actor as president? That's hard to fathom. Next thing you know they'll be a professional wrestler in the White House!

Joe: Try governor.

Danny: Excuse me?

Joe: In Minnesota..... Oh, never mind.

Danny: Have there been any other extraordinary things in the world of presidential politics? That stuff's always interested me.

Joe: Well, since you've been asleep there was one resignation and one impeachment.

Danny: Poor guy. At least he had the integrity to resign. What was his name?

Joe: These were actually two men, Danny. One resigned without impeachment, and the other was impeached without resigning. They were Richard Nixon and Bill Clinton.

Danny: Bill? You call the president of the United States *Bill*? That's a little informal, isn't it?

Joe: Ha! You missed out on Jimmy Carter. Our society has become much more informal in the past three decades. And we seem to have a lot less respect for authority than we used to.

Danny: Yes, I noticed that, just by what I read in the newspapers and have heard on the radio in the past week. And by the way, I thought Vice-President Nixon said he wasn't going to run for political office anymore after losing in that California governor's race.

Joe: I guess he changed his mind.

Danny: And this loss of respect, this cynicism I've been noticing – what do you think has caused it?

Joe: Oh, that probably goes back to the hippies.

Danny: The *what*?

Joe: The hippies. You missed out on the hippies and the yuppies. Hippies came around a couple years after you left. Remember the beatniks? Hippies took their place, coming right after them.

Danny: They didn't like authority?

Joe: They rebelled against it. The late 60s and early 70s was a time of rebellion and change.

Danny: But what did they rebel against and why?

Joe: The establishment. It had to do with the Vietnam War, the Civil rights movement, the women's liberation movement, the assassinations, and of course Watergate.

Danny: What's that last thing – part of a pool deck? A beach? Was there a movement against beaches?

Joe: No, that was an apartment complex in Washington, DC. It had to do with that Nixon resignation thing I was telling you about.

Danny: So, all of these movements and events together caused quite a stir against authority, huh?

Joe: Yup. There were certainly some injustices to fix, but looking back, it seems that one underlying factor undergirding all the protesting was the general opulence of the nation. After World War II, prosperity freed many people from survival mode and provided them with the time and leisure to complain and rebel.

Danny: Interesting assessment, Joe. Boy, I hope one of those 60s hippie people never becomes president. That would be a disaster, wouldn't it?

Joe: Yes, it *is* a disaster. Ask attorney Ken Starr.

Danny: The only Starr I know is Ringo Starr. He didn't run for president, did he? Next thing you'll tell me is that Sonny and Cher became congressmen or something.

Joe: No, just Sonny. And I meant *Ken* Starr, not Ringo. Oh, it's not important.

Chapter 3

The sexual devil-ution

Danny: Sometimes I don't know whether to take you seriously, Joe. So, tell me more about these hippies. What were they like?

Joe: They grew their hair long, often did drugs for fun, began the free-love movement, and talked about peace all the time.

Danny: That sounds nice. Peace is good and love *should* be unconditional. But that drug stuff, I'm not sure how that fits in.

Joe: Danny, what I meant by free love was uncommitted sex.

Danny: *Shhhh!* Joe, there might be ladies around here! Lower your voice when you speak about that kind of thing.

Joe: Oh boy! I almost forgot. You haven't lived

through the sexual revolution.

Danny: *Shhh!* There you go again. Are you trying to embarrass us and get us kicked out of here?

Joe: Talking about sex openly doesn't offend people anymore, Danny.

Danny: Have decent people lost their sense of shame? And what is this revolution you speak of? Sounds like a war.

Joe: In a sense it was. It set off a larger culture war that still persists. The sexual revolution is something that began in earnest right after your disappearance, and it's with us to this day. It's a movement that you could say separates America into two camps, philosophically.

Danny: Well, what is it?

Joe: It was a movement that made people more open about sex, more willing to express themselves sexually outside traditional modes and boundaries.

Danny: What in the world did you just say?

Joe: You know how you're uncomfortable mentioning sex in public? The sexual revolution made sex more open and available, and people more free to experiment in this area of their lives. It's become a lot more acceptable.

Danny: What has? Adultery? Fornication?

Joe: Oh, Danny, we're a little more sophisticated than that now. We just refer to it as extramarital relationships. Everyone is entitled to such a relationship as long as they are consenting adults.

Danny: Joe, you never used to talk like this before. You knew the natural order of God's law doesn't allow for extramarital sex. Is this what the sexual revolution did, make people use euphemisms to rationalize sin?

Joe: Oh, that's another thing. We don't really talk about sin anymore, even in church. We focus more on God's love, mercy, and compassion. Sin and punishment are something people used to dwell on in the past – in your time – but we've pretty much grown out of that.

Danny: Grown out of sin? You mean everyone's become a saint in the 1990s. That's great if it's true.

Joe: It's not that. It's just that we've pretty much gotten past the idea of sin. Since God is love and mercy, it's become pretty much irrelevant to us. He's a forgiving God. And besides, the idea of sin is not good for people's self-esteem. What's really important is to be nice to people.

Danny: Nice? Joe, you just don't sound like the same guy. So let me get this straight. This sexual revolution of the past three decades makes it okay to have sex outside of marriage, but you don't sin unless you're not nice to someone?

Joe: Well, that's simplifying it, but you're on the right track.

Danny: I can't believe people would buy into that

nonsense. Women certainly wouldn't cave to that kind of logic.

Joe: Sorry to shock you Danny, but they have.

Danny: Impossible. Since the dawn of mankind, women have been the guardians of chastity. It's not natural for them to surrender their dignity.

Joe: I'm telling you Danny, they have.

Danny: You mean to say that women are consenting to premarital affairs now?

Joe: In droves. In fact, it's now the exception to the rule for a bride to be a virgin on her wedding day.

Danny: How horrible! The devil has really gotten his claws on us. Everyone used to realize that you can go to hell for sex outside of marriage. And don't these women today care that they're squandering the precious gift of themselves to someone who isn't their husband?

Joe: Apparently not.

Danny: Don't people care about the lasting damage this does to marriage? I can't believe so many are willing to rob each other of this most precious gift meant to be exclusively for one's spouse.

Joe: Not too many people think like that anymore, Danny. We live more in the here and now.

Danny: Not think? The vital significance of exclusive intimacy for marriage is being squandered, and no one thinks about it? Are you sure people just aren't in denial?

Joe: Well, whatever. It's just not an issue anymore.

Danny: It's hard to believe. Marriage has become a joke, then. This lifestyle you speak of completely ignores the nature of the male and female psyche and the meaning of marriage. A man can't cherish his wife as one-flesh if she's already become one flesh with others. And she can't respect him as much for not waiting for her. It seems like the perfect setup for divorce once the challenges of life come knocking. Let me ask you something, Joe. Before I became unconscious, you'd only hear about divorce by reading Hollywood gossip magazines. Have divorces increased?

Joe: They've skyrocketed. Last I heard, one out of every two marriages end in divorce.

Danny: That's what I was afraid of; but inevitable from everything you're telling me. One out of two getting divorced and no one thinks about the ramifications of a fornication society? Obviously, there's a connection!

Joe: Maybe we should change the subject?

Danny: How can people be so blind about giving themselves away outside of marriage? Not only the Bible, but common sense tells us becoming one flesh with others before marriage weakens one's future spousal union. Everybody knows this; or at least they used to. Our fathers' and grandfathers' generations wouldn't have thought of marrying a non-virgin. The special and unique intimacy of becoming one flesh is the natural glue of the marital bond. Joe, is that what this sexual revolution did? It made a person's spouse the last of a string of intimate lovers rather than the only?

Joe: Well, in a manner of speaking, yes. And it's done more than that. It's also opened up public education classrooms to comprehensive sex education. That's a positive thing.

Danny: In public schools? Couldn't that be dangerous? Do the public schools teach morality, the meaning of marriage and sexual intimacy, and the importance of chastity; or do they teach the shallow and destructive message of this 'sexual revolution'?

Joe: They teach them sexual responsibility.

Danny: Oh, good. So, they *do* teach Christian morality.

Joe: No, not exactly. They tell the kids there's nothing wrong with sexual experimentation, as long as they protect themselves.

Danny: From what? What's going to protect them from divine justice? From personal heartbreak? From guilt, shame, and low self-esteem?

Joe: They also teach them that it's okay to be different, and to be proud of their sexual orientation.

Danny: Their *what?* And what do you mean by 'different'?

Joe: You know, it used to be that kids would go so far as to kill themselves if they were gay.

Danny: Joe, that's terrible. These kids need help. But I don't think you're making sense here. Why would *being happy* lead kids to suicide? I don't get it.

Joe: Oh, no, gay doesn't mean happy anymore. It now means homosexual.

Danny: No way. The relatively few people saddled with same-sex attraction disorder stole a wonderful word from the English language for their own agenda? That's sad. And the general population allowed it to happen?!

Joe: I guess so. It just happened. Anyway, high schools are now allowing gay student groups, and cities are allowing gay pride parades. It's all part of that sexual liberation movement we were talking about.

Danny: You can't liberate yourself from your own nature. Liberation begins with freedom *from* sin, not freedom *to* sin. What you're saying is shocking. This perverted behavior is now being taught in public schools as acceptable, and parents aren't storming the schools with pitchforks? Have we lost our minds!? How did this ever come to be!?

Joe: I don't know. It just has.

Danny: Let me ask you another question, Joe.

Joe: Ask away.

Danny: Homosexuality notwithstanding, if all this

extramarital activity you're mentioning is now happening, what happens to all the babies conceived? There must be orphanages everywhere that are overloaded with children!

Joe: To the contrary, one of the most fundamental rights won by women in this sexual revolution has been reproductive rights – her freedom to choose.

Danny: Reproductive rights? I don't get it. Women have always had the right to refrain from the reproductive act. The government hasn't gotten involved in forcing women to reproduce, have they?

Joe: Danny, you're missing the point. Freedom of choice and reproductive rights now refer to having an abortion.

Danny: What! Quiet down Joe, people might hear you. No.... don't tell me.... killing children before birth is now legal? Don't tell me that's true, Joe. It can't be! After modern science in the 19th century proved that human beings begin their lives at conception, abortion became an unacceptable taboo. An unspeakable crime. People haven't gone back to the pagan practice of killing their unborn babies now, have they?

Joe: Danny, I know things were a lot different before you woke up. Yes, women now have the right to an abortion whenever they choose. Statistics say at least a quarter of all women of childbearing age have had at least one abortion. Don't look so shocked. You're turning white.

Danny: When murder becomes legal and acceptable, it's fitting to turn white.

Joe: We don't call it murder or even killing. It's the 'termination of a pregnancy'.

Danny: There you go with euphemisms of denial again. I'm surprised at you. Everyone knows it's the killing of an innocent developing child. I hope these grave injustices are very rare. Joe, this *is* rare, isn't it? You were pulling my leg about those numbers, right? Even if it's legal, women wouldn't actually have their unborn children killed….. would they?

Joe: Well, the last time I heard there had been around 45 million surgical abortions since abortion was legalized by the Supreme Court in 1973. That's 1.5 million a year; around 4,500 every single day.

Danny: You mean to tell me I now live in a world that routinely slaughters unborn babies; and this genocide has been going on since 1973? Joe, this is nothing less than a nightmare. Forty-five million people who should be with us today have been killed before birth!

Joe: Oh, Danny, you're exaggerating, aren't you? You sound like our current pope who calls the Western world a 'culture of death.'

Danny: It seems he's correct. Before I woke up, nobody would even mention the word abortion, and no one in their right mind would ever consider the practice as morally legitimate. Everyone knew it was the killing of an innocent human child. What in the world happened to us?

Joe: Danny, you're just looking at things the way

someone looked at them before the new enlightenment. You'll get used to it.

Danny: Joe, I'm disappointed in you. I hope I don't
become as numb to this depravity as you have. And I
hope I never come to a point of calling evil good with
euphemisms like "enlightenment." Joe, can't you see
the catastrophic evil of this culture of death? I know,
this has all been a farce, right? You wanted to get a
rise out of me, just like you used to do.

Joe: No, not at all. This is what the world has become.
Like it or not.

Danny: But how, Joe? How could this nightmare culture of death have occurred so quickly? Since it's now
1999, we're missing around a third of our people under 27 years old – and are beginning to miss their potential progeny, too. The world is missing a huge
chunk of two generations because of abortion!

Joe: You think too much. I'm not even going to tell
you about partial-birth abortion, which is taking
place due to our latest president's veto pen.

Danny: Hey, it doesn't matter what stage of maturity a child is at when killed. Modern science back in 1965 knew that a human being begins at conception, when a sperm cell mingles with an ovum! After that, stages of development, maturity, and dependence are irrelevant. I'm sorry for raising my voice here, but to say this is an unspeakable disgrace would be a *huge* understatement. Joe, I need to understand two things to wrap my head around all of this: How it's gotten this bad, and why good people like you don't seem to be alarmed about it.

Joe: I'm not sure what to say. I wish I were more of a thinker like you. I kind of just accept things as they come.

Danny: That is very dangerous, for the soul and for the world. It makes sense that a revolution against God and His sixth commandment would create a fornication culture, which would lead to an abortion culture by the demand it creates. But how did it all begin? That's the mystery to me that I'm trying solve. There must have been something behind all this, some catalyst, that enabled this 'revolution' to take off.

Joe: What are you getting at?

Danny: I see the dominoes falling, but I don't yet see the first domino that caused it. Look. In only 35 short years divorce, which was almost unheard of, is now commonplace. The practice of killing unborn children, which was morally unacceptable and extremely rare, now claims the lives of millions of children. Homosexuality, which was known to be a grave perversion of natural law, is now acceptable and even encouraged by the state. And fornication, which was seen as shameful and harmful to the institution of marriage and to children is now the norm. I'm sure there's probably more, but I'm not even going to ask, yet. It's the catalyst, the first material cause, that I'm trying to discern. What about *Playboy*, Joe? Is that nudity magazine still in existence?

Joe: Yes, Danny. But it's considered mild now.

Danny: What do you mean?

Joe: What you used to see in *Playboy* you now see in most movies. Prime time TV constantly depicts premarital sex as normal and acceptable, and hard-core pornography is easily accessible to everyone. You'd be shocked at what you can find with just the click of a computer mouse.

Danny: So, Elvis and the Frankie Avalon–Annette Funicello beach movies are no longer considered risqué?

Joe: Danny, you should go to a beach someday. Women wear nearly nothing.

Danny: But this all fits into the same puzzle within a culture of denial. I mean, how can any society expect to have a low divorce rate, a low out-of-wedlock pregnancy rate, a virtually nonexistent abortion rate, and psychologically healthy young people in this kind of environment? It's an irrational expectation. Anyone who understands human nature knows sexual immorality blinds people to the true and the good, not to mention it militates against marriage and the family.

Joe: What do I know? I'm just a simple computer programmer.

Danny: There has to be something behind all this that I'm missing, a missing piece, a link that got the ball rolling into this abyss. There must be a catalyst to provide the foundation for this so-called revolution that has enabled such a deluge of sin to be unleashed.

Joe: Sin unleashed?

Danny: You're not aware? I'm afraid that living in this environment through the three and a half decades I've been out of commission has your mind conditioned. It makes sense to me that this culture of death you mention must have begun with the sexual revolution you've described. The precepts of the fifth and sixth commandments – sins against human life and sexuality – are intimately related. Disrespecting sex inevitably leads to disrespecting its natural end, human life. Abortion is where illicit sex and violence meet.

Joe: Interesting assessment, Danny. You're still filled with philosophical wisdom after all these years. Furthermore, in addition to all I've mentioned, we now have AIDS.

Danny: For what?

Joe.: Excuse me?

Danny: Helpers for what?

Joe: Helpers? Oh *AIDS*, not helpers ... ah, never mind for now. It's a deadly sexually transmitted disease.

Danny: Again, what puzzles me almost as much as the breakdown of the family and the genocidal abortion culture you describe, is the acceptance and lethargy of people like you—Catholics, who know the truth. Why aren't Catholics and other Christians, as well as all people of good will, deeply alarmed about this?

Joe: Well, I just don't know.

Danny: I just don't get it. Joe, tell me something. All

these women today in the workforce in positions that used to be occupied by men... what happens when they have children? They're staying home until their children are grown and self-reliant – aren't they?

Joe: No, not exactly.

Danny: What do you mean, *not exactly*? If both parents are working, who forms and nurtures the children?

Joe: Well, there are many alternatives in that area today. A lot of people are opting for daycare.

Danny: A lot of alternatives to raising your own child? I'm almost afraid to ask.... Okay, what is daycare?

Joe: Daycare centers are places that mothers drop off their children so that they can go to work. These centers are everywhere now. It's good for the kids to be with other children their own age.

Danny: You mean to tell me that mothers are now

dumping their children off at these centers and picking them up at night, after working a full day? At what age does this start for the child?

Joe: Not all mothers do it. But those that do start their children off at daycare not too long after their birth, maybe a few weeks or a few months. With both parents now working, they're able to provide for the needs of their children. Life isn't easy today you know.

Danny: But Joe, everyone knows the most important thing a child needs is his mother's presence. And to a different degree his father. At least everyone *used* to know this.

Joe: It's quality time that matters now, Danny, not quantity time.

Danny: What? That sounds like another euphemistic saying. And what kind of quality time would an exhausted mother have after working a full day, while having to cook and clean when she got home? Joe, our mothers were home every day for us, and you know how important that was for our sense of security and well-being. I would have been a different person without the family stability my mother's presence offered me.

Joe: Well, it's different now. Women have won their equal rights, so they feel they should practice them.

Danny: At the expense of their children?

Joe: They don't think of it that way. And besides, many of these women have to work in order to make ends meet.

Danny: After observing people's homes and cars in the past week, I just don't believe that to be the case. If a family wanted to do it, most could find a way, like moving into a smaller house, sharing a car, or ridding themselves of the many modern gadgets people have today. By the way, Joe, what most people have today in America makes middle-class families in the 1960s look like they're from a poverty-stricken nation.

Joe: I never thought of that. But everyone owns this

kind of stuff now. You've got to keep up with the times, you know, or you'll fall behind.

Danny: Or maybe you'll *fall ahead*.... Since the times are militating against children and families, trying to keep up with them seems selfish and destructive. Joe, how about the grandparents? Are they an integral part of the family like they used to be?

Joe: Some are. But many decide to move down to Florida. And, of course, many are in nursing homes.

Danny: Nursing homes?

Joe: Oops. I shouldn't have mentioned that.

Danny: So now many grandparents move away from their children and grandchildren to live in a warm climate across the country, while still others are in *what*?

Joe: They're called nursing homes.

Danny: Homes with nurses?

Joe: Something like that.

Danny: So, families don't care for their own elderly anymore?

Joe: I know it sounds cold, Danny, but it's so hard today, especially since so many more women are working outside of the home.

Danny: That sounds like a recipe for disaster. The woman is the glue of the family, without whom it's bound to fall apart.

Joe: They've decided they want more. And they would find your statement sexist.

Danny: What in the world could be more important than that? If children are dropped off at day care and the elderly at nursing homes, how is that 'more'? Have suicide rates increased? I bet there will come a day when teens and the elderly will consider suicide as an option to their pain and emptiness due to the lack of love.

Joe: I hate to admit it, Danny, but teen suicide rates have skyrocketed since you left, and ... well ... for now, let me just mention the name Dr. Jack Kevorkian.

Danny: Dr. *Who*?

Joe: No, not Dr. Who, Dr. Kevorkian. Never mind. You'll find these things out eventually.

Chapter 4

Uncovering the great mystery

Danny: It sounds like the breakdown of the family is still very much underway. Families still get together at least on Sundays, don't they Joe? I mean since it's the day of rest and worship, so I assume families still come together after church.

Joe: Oh, that's another thing that's happened. While fewer people go to church, stores and other businesses are now open on Sundays. And kids often have a sporting event or practice to attend on Sunday mornings. People just don't have time to attend church and visit family like they used to. We're too busy.

Danny: Too busy for God? For each other? There's something I'm missing here. I know there is. I won't rest until I find it.

Joe: What do you mean?

Danny: All of this couldn't have happened so quickly without something radical enabling these dominoes to fall. I may be close, though. Joe, tell me, as I drive through today's neighborhoods I see big fancy houses with nice cars – but no children. Where are all the children? When we were kids, they were everywhere, playing in the woods, climbing trees, playing street hockey, neighborhood baseball, and just visiting each other's houses. Neighborhoods seem sterile now, so dead. Where are all the kids?

Joe: There aren't that many kids anymore. When we were younger, families had 5 or 6 kids, remember? Today, they have one or two. And since neighborhoods aren't filled with children like they used to be, many of their activities have become formalized and institutionalized by adults, and children are being driven all over the place. Boy, Danny, your mode of thinking may be starting to rub off on me.

Danny: Good, Joe. It's important that you see the forest through the trees. Maybe now you can help me figure this mess out – particularly its cause and enabler that has remained elusive to me.

Joe: I don't know what you're looking for, but I'm here for you.

Danny: Whatever it is, I think I'm getting closer. How sad that kids aren't experiencing nature and using their imaginations as they used to. Hmm… only one- or two-child families… Doesn't make sense… Joe, when did this so-called sexual revolution begin?

Joe: I'd say it took off in the late 60s / early 70s.

Danny: I've been unconscious since 1965, so something big must have happened soon afterwards to launch this revolution. It doesn't make sense that all this illicit premarital sex has ultimately produced *fewer* children than when sex was largely reserved for marriage.

Joe: You've got a point.

Danny: Maybe it didn't seem like a major thing at the time, but there must have been something unique, unusual, new that was introduced to society, perhaps particularly to women. Was there anything you can think of that began to change the landscape with regard to sexual morality and marriage?

Joe: I'm not sure what you're trying to get at, but I don't remember anything that might fit that mold.

Danny: I'm not sure either, but using deductive reasoning, I know there must have been something that opened the Pandora's box creating a sea change in people's moral thinking, enabling all this to snowball. Let's think about this. There had to have been *something* to green-light normalizing behaviors that had been universally condemned for several millennia – beginning with sex outside of marriage. Hmm... I have a thought. Other than the obvious religious deterrent, the most *practical* reason for young people remaining chaste before marriage was the fear of pregnancy. Along with fear of parents and, of course, the fear of hell, *fear of pregnancy* kept young people with raging hormones in line. Even those without religious morals. Fear of pregnancy is an appropriate fear since procreation is the natural end of the conjugal act. So, again, I wonder two things... what happened to the natural fear of pregnancy...and where are all the children that should be here?

Joe: Oh, that's easy. That problem has been taken care of by contraception. It's taken the fear of pregnancy away. I failed to tell you because it's become very much a part of the moral landscape today, but the birth control pill for women had become wildly popular beginning shortly after you left. Since then, contraception and sterilization have become part of the norm of sexual relationships.

Danny: It's been taken care of? A contraceptive pill? Popularized? The norm!? ***That's it!!!*** I think we've solved the mystery! *This* may be the answer that I've been seeking to make sense of it all. Are you telling me that there's a pill now for women to take that temporarily sterilizes them – and it's become widespread and seen as morally acceptable?

Joe: Yes.

Danny: And it's used by most couples today?

Joe: Oh yes, married and unmarried alike. They're

even given to high school girls today.

Danny: And most people today see no moral dilemma in using this unnatural contraceptive? Catholics, who know through Church teaching that contraception is a moral evil, have not pushed back with all the force of divine life that Christ has given them?

Joe: No, not at all. In fact, most couples today use something to protect themselves from unwanted pregnancy – Catholic and non-Catholic.

Danny: Then **that's it!** Mystery solved. *That's* the lynchpin I've been looking for; the foundation that undergirds the entire house of cards. Can you see it!?

Joe: We have? It is?? I see *nothing*.

Danny: That's because you have been so conditioned for the past 35 years to accept what the world has gradually normalized. It takes someone like me, who's missed this sexual devil-ution, to see the bigger picture more clearly.

Joe: I think you mean the sexual *revolution*.

Danny: No, I knew what I was saying. Rejecting an essential portion of God's law and accepting all the lies involved in this makes it clear whose game plan we've been following – the devil's. Hasn't the pope come out with any statements against this demonic movement?

Joe: Sure, plenty. As I mentioned before, he calls modern western society *a culture of death.*

Danny: Of course, he does. As I said earlier, sins against the 6th commandment lead to sins against the 5th: illicit sex to illicit violence, fornication to murder (abortion) – a sexual revolution leads to a culture of death. Any post-Christian society making fornication normative will demand abortion. It's inevitable.

Joe: Hmm. Interesting thoughts. You know Danny, at first I just thought you had to be schooled in the ways of our more sophisticated enlightened times. But the more I listen to you the more you're making me think the world's progress may actually be re-gress.

Danny: Thanks, pal. I'm glad you're coming around. Don't get me wrong though, I've noticed good things, too, since I've been back. There seem to be some technological advances that at least have the potential to benefit humanity. And lip service is be-ing paid to respecting the dignity and rights of the individual. But give it a little thought, Joe, look at what has happened to human life and the family in just 35 years:

If children aren't contracepted out of potential existence, they may be aborted before birth. If they're not killed before birth, they may be dropped off at daycare centers. If they're not dumped at daycare there's a very good chance they're living with absent fathers or mothers working outside the home – in a small family and a sterile neighborhood with very few siblings and friends around. That is sad! It seems material goods have replaced children in America as life's primary value.

Joe: Wow! I've never heard it said like that before.

Generalizations, yes, but pretty spot on. And tragic. You used simple language to communicate simple truth. We're just not used to hearing it being that clearly articulated anymore. I think you may be right about those euphemisms of denial you noticed in me earlier.

Danny: And speaking of denial, on a related subject, I bet not too many Catholics frequent Confession anymore like they used to.

Joe: Not surprisingly, you're right again. Catholics don't go to Confession much anymore. I do remember the long lines at our church Confessional every Saturday when we were kids.

Danny: And I bet, as a result, business is booming for secular counselors and psychologists.

Joe: Boy, is *that* true. How did you know? Back before your experiment not too many people went to therapists, did they? Many today seem to replace the Confessional with the therapist's couch. Why do you think that is, Danny?

Danny: It's simple. Man is attempting to be his own god. Why go to Confession if you've rejected the idea of sin? If you were to mention three and a half decades ago any of the things we've discussed here today as becoming normative in America, no one would have believed it. You'd have been ridiculed for reducing a civilization of life into a culture of death. Yet, here we are and there seems to be no alarm, just resignation and acceptance. I'm afraid to say it seems that most people are now spiritually dead.

Joe: Oh my. That rings true. There's such a lack of awareness. That's why hardly anyone goes to Confession anymore; we're not aware of the sin all around us, which we periodically participate in. Danny, you are the John the Baptist of our time! You, who have been "out in the desert" for the past three and a half decades, are able to see with more clarity than those of us who've been immersed in the world in this era of secular and sexual revolutions.

Danny: Speaking of God's prophets, I bet you hardly ever hear about the realities of sin and hell from the pulpit anymore, do you?

Joe: Correct again. We're constantly reminded of God's love and mercy. So much so that people have lost their understanding of the basic moral law. Back when we were growing up God's justice wasn't hidden in catechesis and homilies.

Danny: And it reminded us of the eternal consequences of us not returning God's love. That's hugely important. Pretty frightening, but it kept us in line though, didn't it?

Joe: It sure did. Hell for all eternity as the consequence of our unrepentant choices that reject God's law is a very scary proposition. As Scripture says, "the fear of the Lord is the beginning of wisdom" (Proverbs 9:10).

Danny: I bet all this sin in the air that's masquerading as legitimate 'choice' and 'alternative lifestyle' is taking its toll on people's overall happiness. I mean, if human life is considered so cheap that most people impede conception or exterminate their offspring, what does this do to the sense of meaning and psychological well-being of those born into the world today? If human life isn't graciously accepted as a sacred and inviolable gift from God, such a dearth of love has consequences. I bet many kids suffer from anxiety and depression today.

Joe: It's funny you should say that. Educators and counselors have seen this as a big problem of late. Kids are either extra-hyper or super-lethargic. Perhaps it's the child version of the anxiety and depression many of their parents live with. They're given drugs to fix the problem, when love and security are what're really needed.

Danny: Filling kids with chemicals doesn't fix anything. Think about it – how can you feel good about yourself if you're an option? A 'choice'. The culture-of-death mentality subtly tells kids they're disposable, and that they're not meant to be from all eternity. When many of their peers have been aborted, and it could have easily been them, what other message does it send? It has to seep into the unconscious minds of people living today.

Joe: I've never thought this through. I don't know if

anyone has. In fact, you're now hurting my brain – but in a good way. You're making me see some profound connections, enabling me to realize how shallow and selfish we've become.

Danny: I'm so glad the veil is coming down for you, Joe. I know it's getting late. One more question, if I may. When we were in high school together, kids got in trouble for chewing gum and running in the halls. We could get suspended for it. Should I assume these aren't the worst things young people do in schools today?

Joe: You can surely assume that. I think you might want to sit down for this one.

Danny: Don't worry, nothing you can say now will surprise me. Go ahead, shoot.

Joe: Yes, that's it.

Danny: *What's* it?

Joe: That's what they're doing now. To each other.

They're shooting each other.

Danny: With spit balls and squirt guns?

Joe: No, with bullets. Believe it or not, it's no longer shocking to hear about kids being shot to death in public schools.

Danny: Shocking, but not surprising.

Joe: What do you mean?

Danny: If young people are formed in a cultural environment that subtly teaches life is cheap with no transcendent meaning, can you be surprised that death would follow? And it's going to get worse until we pull out the tree of secular philosophy by its roots.

Joe: Keep talking Danny. I appreciate your insight.

Danny: Okay. If I may go beneath the surface, it boils down to this: Life and love are one. Life is love-giving and love is life-giving. You can't have life without love or love without life. This is because, as scripture says, we are made in the image of God (Gn 1:27) – who *is* Life (Jn 14:6) and Love (1 Jn 4:8). In Him, life and love are one. Whenever we try to separate or split this most fundamental truth of our being, it's like splitting the atom – but much worse. The result of *this* metaphysical explosion has been much more deadly than any nuclear bomb.

Joe: Okay Danny, you've traveled a little deeper than my mind can handle right now. But I can tell you're on to something good here. What I think I hear you saying is that messing with love inevitably leads to messing with life; that when the equilibrium of sex is tampered with, all hell breaks loose. Similar to what you were saying earlier about the linkage between the fifth and sixth commandments. Am I close?

Danny: You are exactly on the right track, my friend. This is precisely why the sexual revolution ends up in a culture of death. And with your help I've discovered the cause that I've been seeking this whole time. The material catalyst that begins and supports this downward spiral to death is contraception. The sexual devil-ution and culture of death began with one tiny pill, the birth control pill, which relates neither to birth nor control. It's modernity's new forbidden fruit of the tree of knowledge, causing death at its consumption (Gn 2:17) – death of unborn babies, the family, marriage, and society, not to mention countless souls. I can't prove this all yet, but my reasoning and spiritual intuition are able to see the connections rather clearly. I thank you for leading us to solving this mystery.

Joe: I did? I think I'm getting it. At least *some* of it.

Danny: You just have to follow reason. The common practice of unnaturally separating sex from procreation or *love* from *life* is the father of this revolution. Begotten of this contraception culture is fornication, for it makes sense that when you separate sex from procreation you'll separate sex from marriage; and the resultant fornication culture will demand abortion. From the look of things, it seems that's exactly what has happened.

Joe: You're blowing my mind.

Danny: Then I'll say more. Contraception is our suicide pill that ruptures humanity's tri-personal image of God – which is Lover, beloved, and love. Since sexual sin spiritually blinds, impeding life impedes faith. Further, instead of man finding his fulfillment in being an instrument of God, he's cut himself off from God, Who is life and love.

Joe: Sounds profound, and I'm slowly getting it. Perhaps this consuming of forbidden fruit is the reason you're noticing many people today as spiritually dead? I'm almost there, Danny. I'm beginning to see how this all fits together.

Danny: I think so. And people seem so oblivious. Contraception as the new fruit of the tree of death is one of the contemporary world's largest roads to hell.

Joe: Strong words, but I understand. Sterilization too, Danny, has become common. Couples are choosing permanent contraception by being sterilized by surgical mutilation.

Danny: You mean like what we used to refer to dogs

and cats as being "fixed"?

Joe: Yes. Now we do it to people. The bottom line is people today demand sex without responsibility.

Danny: Couples are now neutering themselves by mutilating their bodies? You see where this has gone? We're treating people like animals because people see themselves as just animals. What a grave insult to God, who made us in His divine image!

Joe: That brings up another movement, Danny. Animal rights people are now claiming all the earth's sentient species are equal.

Danny: See what I mean! Treat yourself as a beast and act like one, and eventually you'll see yourself that way. See how this is all interrelated? *Catholic* couples would never mutilate themselves this way, by sterilization ... *would they*? I mean, by being Catholic they have *no* excuse for performing self-abusive mutilation.

Joe: Sadly, they do. Catholics in America have become impotent to resist the powerful currents of the world by ignoring the truth and life Christ has given His Church for over two millennia. Most Catholics don't think or act Catholic anymore, and they tend to trust in science rather than God.

Danny: Now, you're sounding like the Joe I used to know!

Joe: It looks like I'm back, thanks to you, my philosopher friend.

Danny: Welcome back to Reality.

Joe: People today just don't seem to think anymore, do we?

Danny: Sin diminishes the power of reason. When faith in the Logos ('reason' in Greek) is diminished, so is *human* reason. This leaves us with passions and emotional responses to the stimuli of the here and now – similar to other animals – leaving us much more vulnerable to sin. In general, it used to be that men by their big-picture rationality would protect women from sin, and women by their keen sense of wisdom and modesty would protect men from sin. Today, it seems no one's protecting anyone. In fact, everyone seems to encourage it. And the ones suffering the most are the children.

Joe: Boy, I think what you're saying is that children are taking the brunt of the false freedom embraced and lived by their parents. Danny, you're turning on an enormous light for me today. By the way, there's one thing I forgot to tell you about the contraceptives of today. Many of them, including the common birth control pill, the IUD, Depo-Provera, the morning after pill, and RU486, abort children at the very beginning stages of their lives.

Danny: How is this?

Joe: When the contraceptive mechanism fails and a child is conceived, they make it impossible for the tiny human being to attach to his mother's uterine wall. Dead offspring are flushed out of the woman's body without her ever knowing she was *with child*.

Danny: Oh boy… how many women use this hormonal cocktail of death?

Joe: Millions. Probably an overwhelming majority

Danny: Things are even worse than I thought. Women who are contracepting are also aborting – without even realizing it? The numbers of innocents killed before birth must number far beyond our comprehension. Are women this ignorant? Do they know what they're doing?

Joe: Some do, and others don't care. Like the entire abortion industry, if money is the primary value, truth and life are sacrificed. There's a lot of money in preventing human beings from coming into being and in killing them if they do. That is, in contraception and abortion. Wow… I feel better now. I feel like I defeated the devil by just speaking the truth with clarity and conviction!

Danny: Good insight, my friend. This seems to be the devil's stronghold today – keeping people from speaking the truth due to cowardice or lack of spiritual and intellectual insight. We've *got* to get this truth out to the world – even though it will offend many and come with great cost to us.

Joe: You're right. And the Church has always been right. The natural moral law ordained by the Creator God cannot change. It is a mortal sin to freely and knowingly engage in contraception, sterilization, premarital sex, or abortion.

Danny: I assume Catholics practicing these moral evils have the decency to refrain from receiving Holy Communion until they've repented and received absolution in Confession.

Joe: I know it's a sacrilege, but your assumptions are incorrect. Many do receive, simply because they don't know any better. Clergy today are intimidated and don't preach these crucial truths. Many use 'pastoral reasons' as their excuse.

Danny: Pastoral reasons? God is gravely offended by what Pope Pius XI called in *Casti Connubii* the intrinsically vicious act of contraception (CC §54), yet, it's 'pastorally sensitive' to remain silent? Thousands of women are inadvertently killing their children before birth with these abortifacients every week, and clergy respond with silence?! Isn't this negligence a form of cooperation with evil on their part? You would think the mass slaughter of innocents would be top priority for every priest, bishop, and layman. There are far greater numbers of child sacrifices performed by Catholics today than there were with pre-Christian pagans… and clergy are remaining silent?! This keeps getting worse. To whom much is given, much will be expected. These silent priests and bishops must be informed of the consequences of their silence, for the sake of their own souls and those under their spiritual care. Jesus was harshest on the religious leaders of His time.

Joe: The thinking today is that you would turn people off if you proclaim the whole truth on faith and morals; especially morals, and especially sex.

Danny: Then the revolution against God and human nature continues to win. Christ didn't relent after telling his disciples they had to eat His body and drink His blood in John chapter six – even though many of His disciples left Him (Jn 6:66). Nor did He relent after His disciples grumbled upon hearing Jesus condemn divorce. How could a pastor of souls in good conscience, then, keep silent and allow all this sacrilege in the Church? Christians are desperately looking for a strong clear voice to guide them, whether they are fully aware of it or not.

Joe: I know Pope John Paul II has constantly urged priests and bishops to proclaim the truth of *Humanae Vitae*; but the deafening silence continues.

Danny: And the body of Christ remains weakened. If clergy preached on these truths there might be an initial drop-off in congregants, but churches would become more fully alive. People need to be challenged. The hard truths are what ultimately attract, especially men, not a watered down version of them. If we the Church don't challenge the world, who's going to do it? But we must be strategic. From what we've uncovered, it's contraception that serves as the material cause of the sexual revolution and the foundation of its subsequent culture of death. If we attack the foundation the whole anti-Trinity tower of Babel will fall.

Joe: It was tried back in 1968, three years after you took your hiatus, by Pope Paul VI in his response to the birth control movement. His encyclical *Humanae Vitae* (On Human Life) reiterated the Church's perennial condemnation of contraception and abortion. He even predicted the devastation that would occur between the sexes if contraception were to become popular. Remember, this was soon after the pill was promulgated and the contraception explosion hadn't fully hit yet. The papal document was meant to put an end to the controversy and stop all debate.

Danny: Then why didn't it put an end to the debate? Actually, I thought *Casti Connubii* by Pope Pius XI in 1930 had put an end to this question. Why was *Humanae Vitae* even necessary, and why didn't it put an end to the discussion?

Joe: To answer your first question, it was necessary because of the invention of the birth control pill.

There was widespread debate, even within Catholic circles, about whether as a non-barrier method it should be deemed morally licit. As for your second question, I am sorry to say that many lay people, theologians, and even priests openly defied the authoritative teaching of the Magisterium.

Danny: Openly defied? On a matter of morality for the universal Church? God, have mercy. The authority of Christ speaks from the Chair of Peter, and the faithful openly defy?

Joe: I know Danny, it sounds terrible. It shows how *un*faithful many of us were. I'm ashamed to admit it, but I was one of those dissenters. In fact, I've dissented until this very day. I didn't understand the magnitude of the evil before this discussion. God must have sent you to me because now I get it. I see the horror. And to think the present pope, John Paul II, has written so much about how it closes couples off to each other, and I just didn't listen.

Danny: There's no time like the present. Christ gave us His sacred teaching authority, the Magisterium, so that we may always know the truths necessary for salvation. Jesus said, "If you love Me you will keep my commandments" (Jn 14:15).

Joe: I know, Danny, and I am painfully sorry to God and His Church. We have become a "comfortable" Church in the past three and a half decades, and I think many of us have squandered our faith. I need to get to Confession, Danny. I need to get there right away before I begin planning how to attack the pervasive darkness that's out there.

Danny: So do I. It's Saturday afternoon. Let's pay this bill and head over to the closest Catholic church. If it's like it was in the mid-sixties, they'll be hearing Confessions now.

Joe: It is, buddy. I know a church right down the road.

Danny: Sounds like a plan. I hope the priest doesn't fall over when I tell him my last Confession was—34 years ago!

Joe: Ha!. But he's going to declare you a saint on the spot after you tell him only a month's worth of sins!

Danny: I see you haven't lost your sense of humor, Joe. By the way, after this, do you want to help me explain all of this to my family?

Joe: Explain what? What's happened to you *or* what's happened to the world? I think the latter is actually *more* incredible.

Danny: About our culture of death of course, and the grave obligation we all have in doing something to counter it, and ultimately defeat it. If we can convince people of this, then convincing them about what's happened with me should be a piece of cake!

Joe: Hmm... Good point, my friend. Very good point!

Part 2

1999 Meets 2024

**From a Culture of Death
to an Age of Insanity**

Chapter 5

A second welcome back

Back at their favorite restaurant in 1999, several weeks after their last encounter.....

Danny: Joe, I'm happy to have a friend like you who gets it.

Joe: Gets what?

Danny: One who's able to see through the world's lies and judge things objectively.

Joe: That's the grace of God blessing us with an eternal perspective; and fruit of having you as a friend.

Danny: It's seeing reality as it is. Hey, speaking of reality, or tampering with it, I got an official telegram from the Feds today inquiring as to whether I knew of anyone who'd be interested in considering a new program they're implementing.

Joe: New program? What do you mean?

Danny: It's similar to the one I went through. They'd like to freeze another person, this time for a quarter century, in order to test out some new advances in technology.

Joe: Wow! Again? You're not considering it, are you?

Danny: No, I've had my excitement for a lifetime.

Joe: I've been meaning to ask you. Have you been having any serious side effects from your experience?

Danny: No, other than the ignorance that comes with missing out on some precious earth years and having the burden of keeping it a secret from everyone, knowing no one would believe me. Oh, and the pain of knowing people I loved have aged 34 years while I remained the same.

Joe: It's an amazing experience you've gone through, waking up 34 years in the future. It's something you only read about in science fiction novels and dream about in the imagination.

Danny: Yeah, who'd have thought that I'd be the one experiencing science fiction as science fact.

Joe: You know, my wife has passed, my kids are on their own, and I've been feeling a bit stagnant in my job lately.

Danny: Oh? You're not considering this... are you?

Joe: Well, I don't have much to lose. I just might think about it.

Danny: Joe, you love science as much as I do. Although I'd greatly miss you, it could be an opportunity for you to participate in the advancement of humanity in a unique way.

Joe: There would be a lot to consider.

Danny: A warning though; your kids would be around your age when you wake up. You'd have to get used to being the same biological age as them if you did this.

Joe: That would be strange. As you've experienced, a lot would be strange. And exciting, too.

Danny: Hey, if you're at all serious about this, why don't you and your two kids come over Saturday night for the big game. We could all talk about the positives and negatives of the cryonics experience.

Joe: I don't know. I doubt I'll give this idea a second thought. Besides, Jonathan's going to be out at some concert that night and Wendy, well, maybe I could take my daughter Wendy. She likes football, you know. *And* she's a Dolphins fan, like you.

Danny: Really? It's uncommon to find a woman who's into watching football, let alone one that's a Dolphins fan. Sure, come on down. I'd be happy to meet her. If she takes after her dad, she's pretty special.

25 years later, in 2024, at the same restaurant/bar......

Joe: Hey, stranger.

Danny: No way! Is that you, Joe?

Joe: Yes, I'm back! Back to the future, I might say. I'm glad our old haunt here still exists.

Danny: Welcome to 2024, my man! It's good to see you! I thought your return might be this month, but wasn't sure. You look great!

Joe: Yes, it looks like you've almost caught up to me in age. Just a ten-year gap now. Good to see you!

Danny: I assume you went through all your protocols for release, and got a little food and exercise to get you jump-started?

Joe: Yeah, they kept me in the hospital for a few days for observation, and the Feds rented a place for me to live a few miles across the river until I get on my feet again. But I'm fine. How've you been?

Danny: Great. Lots to catch up on. I assume you haven't sought out your family.

Joe: Not yet. This is the first place I've gone.

Danny: Have you been debriefed about the contemporary world of 2024?

Joe: All I know for sure is that Senator Biden from Delaware is now president. I never thought that could happen.

Danny: Have a seat, my friend. Before I divulge something of my personal life that I know will surprise you, I'll do for you what you did for me 25 years ago when I woke up to a whole new world. (To the waiter): We'll have a couple house beers and an appetizer of potato skins. So, where do we begin?

Joe: How about at the beginning? When I left, not too long after that fun night we had over your house with my beautiful daughter Wendy, everyone was worried about the technological disaster Y2K was going to bring. Did the world shut down as feared? Was there any of the predicted chaos?

Danny: None. It came and went without a hitch. Apparently, the world's computers cooperated. No reported problems.

Joe: Wow. A false alarm. I figured there was a bit too much hysteria about that.

Danny: Yup.

Joe: Let's stay with politics for a moment. Before I went into hibernation, Vice President Gore was on the verge of winning the Democratic nomination from Sen. Bill Bradley of New Jersey; and on the other side John McCain and President Bush's son were battling it out for the GOP nomination. How did these primary races end up?

Danny: Great memory. Well, maybe not so great since that was only like last month for you. Twenty-four years ago, in the year 2000 Al Gore did end up beating out Senator Bradley, and after South Carolina's primary, George W. Bush pulled away from

John McCain and ended up with the GOP nomination.

Joe: Well, to my mind Bill Clinton is president. So, who was his successor, Gore or Bush?

Danny: Well, thanks to hanging chads, the Supreme Court had to decide it.

Joe: Hanging who? And Danny, even I know the Supreme Court doesn't decide elections. We learned that in fourth grade.

Danny: It did this time, for all intents and purposes. There had been a great dispute as to who had really won. It ended up in court.

Joe: A dispute? How? The presidency is always decided the night of the election. This one wasn't?

Danny: Very different. To make a very long story short, Florida had a hard time interpreting its vote, and there was a major dispute between the political parties. Florida's electoral votes were the difference in the election.

Joe: Who was this 'Chad' you mentioned? Was he the secretary of state?

Danny: Chad? Oh, the hanging chads. That related to the kind of ballots they had in Dade County and how they were punched and counted. It was a mess.

Joe: So, in the end who won the presidency?

Danny: Bush. And he ended up serving two terms.

Joe: Wow. His father must have been proud. By the way, I happened to take a train through New York City yesterday. Maybe I was just tired or distracted, but I could have sworn the World Trade Center twin towers were missing. Very strange. But maybe I was just looking in the wrong place.

Danny: You're not crazy, Joe. The twin towers are no more. They were taken down by terrorists.

Joe: What?! How is that even possible?

Danny: By flying airplanes into them. It was a suicide mission pulled off on September 11, what we came to call 9/11, by Arab Muslim terrorists to send America some kind of message. At least that's the official story we got. Almost 4,000 people died in that tragedy.

Joe: That's much worse than what happened at Pearl Harbor.

Danny: That same day two other suicide flights were headed for the Capitol building and the Pentagon. The latter was successful in crashing into the building. More Americans died in the horror.

Joe: Unbelievable! Did it start World War III?

Danny: Not quite. But it got America into a quagmire in Iraq and Afghanistan for many years.

Joe: Unbelievable. I'll get all the details from you on that later. Amazing. Anything else extraordinary occur while I was gone?

Danny: The nation got its first black president.

Joe: Wow! Let me guess. Jesse Jackson may have been too passé. Did Bill Cosby get into politics after his hit prime-time show? He was universally respected at the time I had left.

Danny: No, he won himself a term in the jailhouse, not the White House. But that's a long story that I still don't fully understand.

Joe: Was it Alan Keyes? He was a spitfire. Maybe Michael Jordan got into politics after his career ended?

Danny: No, the first black president was Barack Hussein Obama.

Joe: Who? A guy with that name became president after the terror attack by Muslim extremists? Interesting. I'll have to look him up. What about Bill Clinton's wife? I know she had high ambitions. Did she ever run?

Danny: Oh yeah. Twice. She lost to Obama in the 2008 primaries and to Donald Trump in the 2016 general election.

Joe: Donald Trump? The New York real estate developer and millionaire playboy – who no one took seriously? That's not possible.

Danny: Some unpredictable things have happened over the past two and a half decades.

Joe: I guess so. It seems everyone now has one of those mobile car phones on them. Are they commonly used now?

Danny: Cell phones – yes, everyone has one now, for phone calls, texting, taking pictures, and the internet.

Joe: You can actually get the internet from one of those little mobile phones? Wow. They're like minicomputers! And what do you mean by "texting".

Danny: You can send people messages on their phone now without calling them.

Joe: Oh, like pagers. Hey, don't look now, but why is that woman over there wearing that doctor's mask on her face? I thought I saw a few other people wearing something similar the other day on their faces in a grocery store. Has this become a new fad or fashion statement?

Danny: I wish it was only that, Joe. COVID-19 changed the world several years ago. I'm glad for your sake you missed it.

Joe: Covid 19? Sounds like a robot. Does everyone now have robots in their homes?

Danny: No, not yet, but they're working on that.

Joe: Any general movements on the international scene with liberal Joe Biden as president?

Danny: Well, his Democratic Party has clearly become the Party of Death, and seems to be gradually going socialist.

Joe: Socialist? The Democratic Party is going socialist? I never thought I'd live to see a major political party in the United States of America go in the direction of socialism.

Danny: Me neither. But that's what the breakdown of the family has caused – a vacuum of patriarchy that's being usurped by the government. It's all part of the plan. Hey, speaking of family, I want to introduce you to my wife, whom I married exactly one year after that shindig we had at my house that final night we were altogether. She's coming over right now. I think you'll find she looks pretty familiar. (Looking to his right and waving) Honey, over here.

Joe: Wendy!!

Wendy: Dad, it's really you!

(Both tightly hug each other while sobbing.)

Joe: You look amazing for fifty!

Wendy: Thanks for reminding me, Dad. And you look so young. What are you biologically, now, around 60? I missed you so much!

Joe: I'm 59. Same as when I fell asleep, which seems like last week to me. Hey, I'm not too much older than you two biologically.

Wendy: Did Danny tell you?

Joe: Tell me what, that he was married? Yes. Danny, you said she was on her way. I look forward to meeting her.

Danny: You already have. (Danny and Wendy embrace.)

Joe: Huh? What? You mean… You two!

Danny: Yes! We fell in love shortly after you introduced us at my house 25 years ago – which is last week for you!

Wendy: Yes, Dad, we had such a good time that night he asked me to dinner the following week. Then he really helped me in a lot of ways after you departed.

Joe: You two are married!?

Danny: I hope you don't mind, Joe. I'd have asked

for your blessing, but you were in hibernation.

Joe: Mind? I'm overjoyed! This is great news! Wow. Any kids?

Wendy: We've got three – 21, 18, and 16. And Jonathan has two kids, too! You're a grandfather of five now!

Joe: I can't wait to meet them all. Sit down, Wendy. Danny, ah, *your husband*, has been debriefing me about some of the major occurrences of the past 25 years. Maybe you can help him out.

Wendy: Sure, I'll give it a shot.

Joe: This is *SO* exciting. My daughter is married to my best friend, who's my age, but her age simultaneously. We are truly living the stuff of science fiction! *Okay*, Danny, you were telling me about our government leaning socialist and mentioned something about a grand plan.

Danny: Yeah, but I don't think it's just our government. It's international. We seem to be getting closer to a one-world government when there will be centralized banking, centralized health care, and international law directed by the United Nations and its affiliates. The problem is that these organizations have all become secular progressive in their thinking. In other words, atheists.

Joe: The U.S. is giving up its sovereignty? Allowing secular humanist forces to redefine our values? That is terrible news.

Danny: It seems to be going that way. And much of the social engineering is based on a misogyny that the contemporary world calls "women's rights." The Left is ingenuous in knowing how to manipulate the masses.

Wendy: Yes, it's gotten progressively worse since you've been gone, Dad. The sexual revolution, which was simply a way of rebranding the abuse of women with impunity, has fooled so many of us women.

Joe: It's gotten even worse, huh?

Wendy: It's savage. I was so blessed to find Danny when I did. I think he saved me from years of heart-break and disappointment.

Joe: I vouch for that. The moral character of Danny is rare, and what every father wants for his daughter.

Danny: Thanks, Buddy.

Joe: Hey, I've learned a lot from you. You've got the wisdom of Solomon, with a lot fewer wives.

Danny: Ha, Wendy's all I need.

Joe: Danny, speaking of women, I noticed a violent sport on TV in which people seem to be trying to kill each other, called kickboxing or ultimate fighting, or something along those lines.

Danny: That's become as popular as regular boxing. And, yes, it's pretty violent.

Joe: I'm surprised it's even legal. But I was most shocked that women were involved in this violent so-called sport. And everyone seems to be okay with it! It's hard to believe people now enjoy watching women kicking and punching each other into oblivion. In 1999, women were fighting for equal rights; now they're fighting each other like animals. I found it shocking. What real man, or woman for that matter, would sit there and enjoy watching two women seriously hurt each other?

Danny: They've made abuse of women into an art, Joe – whether it be with sex or violence – and they justify it by using terms like "adult consent" and "adult entertainment."

Wendy: Yes, Dad, it's pretty gross. The fruit of the revolution, begun 60 years ago with the promulgation of 'the pill,' has led women to lose sight of true womanhood. They must choose one of two extremes: become counterfeit men or authentic whores. This is what's left after the contraception revolution and its sterilizing effect rejected true womanhood.

Joe: You're sounding more like your husband; and I like it.

Wendy: I'm flattered, but it's true. You can't convince women for a half century to be on artificial hormones that counteract femininity and what it means to be a woman, and expect there to be no deleterious results. That's why #MeToo came to be, but can never bring about justice: It emphasizes only injustices against women when there is no consent.

Joe: Hold on Wendy, I don't understand. *You too* can never bring about justice? What injustice are you seeking to bring about?

Wendy: No, no, not *me too*, but #MeToo, the movement. I'll fill you in on that later, but let's just say much of society is abusing women, but it's considered abuse only when the woman is smart enough to realize it's abuse. And this on the whole is rare. The elites have redefined abuse of women in order to continue it, all in the name of women's rights. It's very sad to behold.

Chapter 6

The war on men and the death of reason

Joe: This is very sad. The masculinization of women was already well underway when I went into hibernation, beginning in earnest with the chemical-hormonal poison of the birth control pill. But I'm noticing women have become even more masculine of late, *and* men are becoming more feminine. Is this just my imagination?

Danny: Tell me about it.

Joe: Every time I see men on TV – and I love your flat-screen TVs now – they're portrayed as goofy, feminine, or idiotic. That nonsense had already started before I went into hibernation, but what's different now is that I hardly see men at all in commercials. Particularly white men. And whenever I do, they seem to be effeminate or blatantly homosexual. What's with this?

Danny: The Leftist elites would deny this, but there's

an obvious attempt at social engineering among the corporate-government class and media in this country. Since you haven't been around, you can see it more clearly. Have you noticed the transgenders?

Joe: The trans *what*?

Danny: The newest movement in our age of insanity is called *transgenderism*. It's the latest jaunt into the world of 'progressive' ideology.

Joe: Transgenderism? I have no idea what that means, but I know the word gender refers to masculine and feminine nouns in many of the world's great languages. Is this a trend to bring English in line with the other languages that gender their nouns?

Danny: That's what gender used to mean. These languages reflected the universal principles of masculinity and femininity, and applied them to objects in the material world. But this is different. Just as the secular Left stole "gay" from its common meaning of being *happy*, they've taken "gender" and confused it with *sex*. Now everyone's confused.

Joe: Come again? The word now refers to changing one's sex as male or female?

Danny: Well, yes and no. This is the genius of the progressive Left. Their leader from hell is very cunning. His instruments, the Leftist cultural elites, have created an ambiguity between the terms sex and gender in order to convince the masses to use sexed pronouns for the "gender" that people *identify* with – not the sex that they actually are. Now, supposedly, one's so-called gender can be the opposite of one's sex.

Joe: Huh? Are you serious? They've confused sex and gender and have convinced people they can be contrary to each other? As we discussed before I left, there was a similar rupturing of life and love when they foisted contraception on the populace in the 1960s and 70s. To deconstruct being and goodness is the *modus operandi* of the Devil. It's a way of maintaining a culture of death.

Danny: Very wise, Joe. In addition to this craziness, some are saying there are now hundreds of genders.

Joe: Before I even attempt to wrap my head around that nonsense, why do you keep using the word "progressive"? Are liberals now calling themselves progressives?

Danny: Sometimes, I take things for granted. Yes, the great cultural divide between secular humanism and Christendom is now often referred to simply as progressive and conservative.

Joe: But "progress," which is the root word of progressive, is a neutral term. Its value depends on what one is progressing *toward*. Cancer and tooth decay are progressive, and obviously aren't good. Do these so-called progressives make clear what they are progressing toward?

Wendy: Not at all, Dad. Ambiguity is the invaluable tool of the Left. As long as you're not clear and don't appeal to the higher rational part of human nature, you can more easily manipulate people according to their emotions and passions. I think, however, from all indications, their aim is to "progress" past God and His universal moral law.

Joe: Progressing past God? Becoming one's own gods? This reminds us of original sin as illustrated in Genesis 3:5-6, doesn't it?

Danny: This kind of pride is the grandfather of all sin: seeking to be one's own god. That way you can create your own reality and morality and fool yourself into believing you're in charge.

Joe: But from what you're both saying, and from the snippets of info that I've been able to piece together in the past couple of weeks, I see a scenario where the powerful corporations are in cahoots with government, especially Democrats. Unless people are firmly grounded in God's truth, they don't have a chance.

Danny: True. Only the light of Christ can save us.

Joe: Can I explore this new "transgender" movement, as they're calling it, a little further? Some things in my day were evil and vicious, like the advent of the abortion age and the divorce culture; but this is different. Those were born of a selfish desire for apparent goods. Sex and love are morally good when practiced in right order. But this seems to be outside the realm of sanity of selfishness. No one in their right mind could ever buy into this idea that a biological man is a woman if he declares it so.

Danny: Many have, Joe. There aren't as many "right minds" anymore. Common sense has become pretty uncommon. It's the continued legacy of the sexual revolution. Remember the principle that illicit sex spiritually blinds.

Joe: No question. The so-called "gay rights" movement was one blatant example of that.

Danny: And that's now part of the alphabet soup movement.

Joe: The what?

Danny: They're now attempting to justify the full gamut of objective sexual disorders under one acronym: LGBTQI+. The '+' indicates it keeps growing.

Joe: How can you ever remember that?

Wendy: And, Dad, the Supreme Court has gotten more involved in upholding sexual perversion. Do you remember that so-called right to privacy that it conjured up from the liberty clause of the Constitution to justify crimes against nature? It's become the legal magic bullet to blow away any laws remaining that uphold common decency in society. You remember how Justice Kennedy put it back in the 1992 decision of *Casey vs. Planned Parenthood*: "At the heart of liberty is the right to define one's own concept of existence, of meaning, of the universe, and of the mystery of human life."

Joe: I can't say I'm surprised. Modern philosophy has redefined liberty to mean license. Has the high court ruled against sodomy being a crime against human nature?

Wendy: Yes, but more than that. Not only did the high court strike down Texas' anti-sodomy laws in 2003... I think you'd better sit down for this one, Dad. The Supreme Court in 2015 ruled in favor of so-called same-sex "marriage". There are now countless people with same-sex attraction disorder legally "married" in the United States.

Joe: That's hard to believe. We have absolutely lost our minds. Another domino falling to the contraceptive mentality, which conditions people to believe sex is not necessarily linked to procreation, as essence is to end. But once violating natural law becomes the norm, as it has been with the acceptance of the seismic rupture between the unitive and procreative significance of sexual love, it rationalizes all sexual perversions. What you're telling me now is just another example of contraception's legacy in a post-Christian society. It took exactly 50 years for the moral logic of the high court's *Griswold vs. Connecticut* ruling in 1965 to trickle down to legitimize this farcical homosexual "marriage" construct in 2015.

Danny: You are so right. Moral principles seem to have a certain poetic logic to them, don't they? And the insanity is progressing at such a rapid rate that executives in California have gotten fired for having voted against so-called same-sex marriage in its state's referendum.

Joe: It seems civilization may be heading south at a more rapid pace than I remember. Tell me some good news, guys. Have there been any significant happenings of the past 25 years that uphold truth and goodness?

Danny: Here's a piece of good news for you – and it, too, includes a 50-year motif. *Roe vs. Wade* has finally been overturned. It happened in July of 2022.

Joe: Praise the Lord! I was hoping that would happen before I came back to consciousness. That's great news! How many preborn children have been saved because of this? Any idea?

Danny: That's a little tricky. Chemical abortions have become common, even more so than surgical ones. It's been demonstrated since your departure that hormonal pills, including the common birth control pill, act as abortifacients. So, statistics would just be guesstimates.

Joe: It's been *proven* now that contraceptive pills cause abortion?

Wendy: Yes. Scientific studies have confirmed that these pills fail to contracept a certain percentage of the time. When this occurs, the hormonal cocktail within the pill makes the woman's uterine lining impossible for the tiny human being to attach to. It's reasonable to say that, by virtue of this backup mechanism, countless women are having abortions without even knowing it.

Joe: That sickens me, as I'm sure it does the women on the pill after finding this out. So, let me get this straight. So, you're saying surgical killings have continued since I've been out of commission, and chemical abortions have even outnumbered them. This means we're still mired in a culture of death – 50 years after Roe.

Wendy: And we haven't even mentioned the millions of preborn babies killed each year from in vitro fertilization. The number of tiny human beings deliberately killed after purposely creating excess embryos – and all those being kept in freezers around the country – is exponentially greater than the innocents murdered each year in abortion.

Joe: (Silence) Staggering. I can hardly speak. But with the end of Roe, the abortion fight has gone back to the states. Doesn't this cut down on the numbers of child-murder victims?

Danny: In some states, yes. But after 50 years, Roe has created a dependence on abortion.

Wendy: Yes, and women thrust into the demon-inspired premarital sex culture without the supernatural faith to resist it are too fearful of pregnancy ruining their opportunities. Men have become addicted to sex, and women dependent on abortion.

Chapter 7

The snowball effect
of contraception's legacy continues

Joe: We truly are a post-Christian pagan nation.

Danny: No question. But other formerly Christian nations have also been led down this demonic road. Venezuela, for example, recently voted to legalize abortion; and formerly Catholic Ireland in separate referenda voted for abortion and sodomitic marriage. The Devil's claws seem to be everywhere now.

Joe: It reminds me of the Scripture passage Luke 18:8, where Jesus expressed concern about His return at the end of history: "When the Son of man comes, will he find faith on earth?"

Wendy: Oh, it gets worse, Dad. We're just beginning. Drag queens for children are the popular thing now.

Joe: Wait a minute… Speaking of that, I saw a guy on TV the other day pretending to be a woman. I thought it was a joke. There were even headlines about him winning a medal in some women's sport. I laughed it off as a Saturday Night Live-type of skit.

Wendy: It was no joke, Dad.

Joe: Impossible! There's no way we've gone that far down the road of insanity as to let men pretending to be women win medals in women's sports.

Danny: We have. Post-Christian America has entered an age of insanity. Remember, sexual sin distorts the intellect.

Joe: Are women also pretending they're men?

Danny: Yes. Do you remember Sonny and Cher's kid, Chastity Bono? Ellen Page is probably after your time.

Joe: Sonny and Cher's daughter thinks she's a man?

Danny: Yes. And there's Caitlyn Jenner.

Joe: Who's that? Another woman thinking she's a man?

Danny: No, the other way around. Olympic Gold medal decathlon winner Bruce Jenner now identifies as a woman – and the entire media establishment refers to him as a woman.

Joe: What! The top male athlete in the world in the 1970s now parades around as a woman?

Danny: Yes. Even the so-called conservative media outlets refer to him as "she".

Joe: No! The world has turned into an insane asylum in the past 25 years! It's like the elites are claiming two and two equals five and the people are accepting it!

Danny: Pretty much.

Wendy: And that's not the worst of it. Appallingly, genital mutilation for children is becoming more and more common.

Joe: Mutilating children!? Parents would *never* allow money-grubbing doctors to mutilate their kids! Nor would the law allow it!

Wendy: They do and they have. It's almost becoming an epidemic. Parents are allowing their children to be permanently mutilated because these kids are going through a phase that they will most likely outgrow.

Joe: Parents are in on this? Outrageous! Absolutely demonic. But again, I guess I shouldn't be surprised. If a nation murders millions of its children *before* birth, it's not surprising it would mutilate them *after* birth. And if the state allows the slaughter of preborn children, they'd certainly allow the mutilation of born children. The logic is not inconsistent.

Danny: It's certainly morally abhorrent, but it's also embarrassing. We now have an open sodomite serving as head of the transportation department and a so-called transgender man pretending to be a woman serving in Health and Human Services. And you should see some of the extremely *woke* recruitment videos the defense department made to attract recruits. Countries not infected by leftist progressivism must think we're nuts.

Joe: Go a little slower, my friend, with the new labels. I get now what *progressive* means, but why mention making videos with people who are awake? Is making commercials asleep a new trend?

Danny: Point well taken. No, *woke* now refers to extreme political correctness.

Joe: Well, with the military going soft, the economy tanking, and the insanity you've detailed, it seems like I've *awoken* to a nightmare.

Wendy: And this woke stuff Danny's mentioning is a veiled attack on free speech. It's getting to the point where public dissent against the official narrative is squelched; and anyone who crosses the PC-woke line is immediately canceled.

Joe: Canceled? You mean people are killed for speaking against the regime today? This kind of barbarity has come to America?

Danny: No, not yet. Right now, we're only at the point of white martyrdom. People's jobs, reputations, and dreams are being killed.

Wendy: And government is becoming too intrusive. Just look at what happened during the pandemic. Not only were there unnecessary lockdowns and pressure to take experimental vaccines, but government and big tech worked in tandem to squelch all dissenting voices, even those of qualified medical professionals.

Joe: It's all a bit overwhelming.

Danny: Tell me, Joe, since you've been awake have you noticed any other significant differences?

Joe: In my little research on the arts, I've noticed there seems to be very little creativity. Lots of remakes of movies and TV shows made back in the 50s and 60s.

Danny: Oh, you mean like *Superman*, *Batman*, and *The Avengers*?

Joe: Yes, and others. They're just poor remakes of ideas that were born from yesteryear, but with flashier technology. And modern art in general seems to reflect the ambiguity and confusion of the times. And it's just so ugly.

Danny: Ha! Ugliness certainly seems to be a hallmark of our times. Truth, goodness, and beauty – the three transcendental properties of all things reflecting the divine essence – have been attacked in academia, ethics, and art respectively. They're hated from the pits of hell to the cultural Left.

Joe: And that's probably *because* they reflect the infinite and eternal truth, goodness, and beauty of God.

Danny: Bingo.

Joe: I've also been hearing of this thing called artificial intelligence. What is it? Is this something that's been filling the void created by the dearth of human intelligence?

Danny: You might have something there.

Joe: But what does it mean? We know intellect is a spiritual power that we can't replicate. Are there robots now that supposedly think for themselves?

Danny: That's the idea. But despite what some claim, we're not there and never will be.

Joe: I would imagine it could become a dangerous tool, though.

Danny: No question. Some are predicting artificial intelligence could spell the end of humanity.

Joe: So, amidst all the lack of sanity, where is the Church? Although it seems people are rejecting God in droves, at least the Church and her moral authority is respected by the secular world. No?

Danny: Not so much anymore, Joe. That's another thing you've missed. The Church has been mired in scandal since you left. Right after your hibernation began, an investigative report from the *Boston Globe* called 'Spotlight' uncovered a lot of shady and abusive happenings in the Boston Archdiocese. Gradually other scandals came to light across the nation and internationally.

Joe: Scandals? When I left the only scandal within the Church that I sensed was the scandal of silence—silence from the pulpits in the midst of the great secular and sexual revolutions that systematically destroyed countless souls. The clergy will have to answer for that.

Danny: Yes, I certainly concur that the scandalous silence from the pulpit and religious education classes has been deafening. This, by the way, is still the norm at most parishes. But there have been more concrete public scandals since you've been gone.

Joe: What kind?

Danny: Sexual abuse among clergy. The mainstream media has labeled it pedophilia and has convinced the public. But they're lying.

Joe: Then what other kind of sexual abuse has been uncovered within the Church?

Danny: Homosexual abuse. Some eighty percent of the victims of clergy abuse have been post-pubescent males. Yet, while the great majority of victims are young adult males, the media continues to pound the drum that it's pedophilia rather than homosexuality.

Joe: This is disgusting. It's hard to believe sodomites would want to lead a Church that officially condemns the activity. And why do you think the secular establishment powers are shifting the real problem? Both abuses of pedophilia and sodomy are abominations, aren't they?

Danny: One possible answer might be that the normalization of homosexuality is part of the "progressive" agenda, to mock God and dethrone Him in society. Pedophilia is still a taboo, even to the Left, albeit many in the so-called LGBTQ+ community would like to see that change.

Joe: But with regard to homosexuality in the Church, doesn't the Church specifically have an official rule that those with predominant same-sex attraction cannot be accepted into seminaries or ordained as priests?

Danny: Yes! The 1961 rule was clearly confirmed by Pope Benedict XVI in 2005. The pope officially declared that no man saddled with predominant same-sex attraction can be ordained. It explained that even if they're not practicing the unnatural acts, they lack the capacity to relate to men and women in a healthy way.

Joe: Then why are there homosexual priests? Why have men with same-sex attraction been ordained? It doesn't make sense. Has the Vatican disciplined the bishops whose grave transgression allowed for this fatal slip?

Danny: Not that I know of. It's a mystery as to why the Vatican has apparently been lax on this. Not only is ordaining same-sex attracted men disobedient to the authority of Christ given to the pope, but it also results in weakened clergy and public scandal. Even though the Church can never officially teach error in matters of faith and morals, her moral authority in the minds of many can be weakened by scandal.

Joe: Have other organizations had this kind of problem with such natural law violations?

Wendy: Oh, yes. Boy Scouts of America, public school teachers, and daycare centers are just a few examples. It's logical that a society that sells sex in a variety of ways would form people to have unhealthy views and habits with human sexuality.

Joe: So true. But nonetheless, I can understand why people have a particular problem with the Church succumbing to these sins. The Church is the God-appointed instrument to teach and preach the truth about sexual morality.

Danny: No question. There's that, as well as the Luciferian media pouncing on the scandal for their own deleterious agenda.

Joe: Boy, between the deafening silence, and the homosexual infiltration, Christ's mystical body on earth has been weak for decades. The world has no chance of restoring civilization if the Church doesn't follow her divine Head. If Catholics were Catholic, the world would be transformed.

Danny: And that is the tragedy. As they say, to whom much is given, much will be expected. Generally speaking, Catholics will probably be judged most harshly on Judgment Day.

Joe: Sounds right. It's so sad that the human element of the Church has been corrupted in this way. You've both offered me much to chew on. It's pretty exhausting. How about giving me one more bit of *good* news before I head home for the night?

Danny: Okay. Despite all the efforts to destroy the Church from within and without, the Church still stands. And there are still converts entering the Church every Easter vigil. It's a miracle of grace that despite all the real corruption and negative propaganda, converts are still coming home to the Catholic Church. They're still able to see it as the only real alternative to the world and the way to eternal life.

Joe: That *is* excellent news! As they say, where sin abounds, grace abounds even more. While the devil seems to be winning the battles, grace enables many to see that the Catholic Church, which was established upon the apostles by Christ Himself, is the Noah's Ark of the New Covenant that will survive the storms of the world's turmoil until the lighthouse of Christ brings her home.

Danny: That's a nice way of putting it, Joe. Seems like you've been gifted with a fair amount of that wisdom you used to claim I possessed. God is good.

Joe: When you retreat as I did for 25 years, you're not as blinded by the ways of the world when you return. One thing we can both say about our experiences is that our nation has gone from *a civilization of life* to a *culture of death* to an *age of insanity* in less than 60 years. This great fall, as you so deftly articulated to me 25 years ago, has been set in motion by consuming modernity's new forbidden fruit, the birth control pill, which opened the Pandora's box to a *new* culture of death ("If you eat of it you will surely die" [Gn 2:17]). From "the pill" to sexual license, to killing the innocent unborn, to insanity, Western society has been in a downward spiral of destruction from which only God can save us.

Wendy: That's so true, Dad. *Very* sad, but beautifully articulated.

Danny: I concur, Joe. And if we are to be His instruments we need to be faithful and courageous. We need to talk more, the three of us, about our spiritual game plan. But right now, we need to get home to *your* grandkids – who, by the way, look pretty similar to their grandfather.

Wendy: Yes, Dad. But first come down for dinner on Thursday, and I'll invite Jonathan and his family. We'll all catch up.

Joe: Great idea.

Danny: Give us your new phone number and we'll give you a call. We've got much more to cover. Do you do have a cell phone now?

Joe: Yes, I've purchased one of the new mobile phones. It's pretty amazing what it can do. By the way, among other things I've been dying to know who won the 1999 World Series. It was about to begin before I went into my hibernation, but I'll wait. It was so good seeing you two! You give me hope.

Danny: Thanks, my friend. Until next time, enjoy learning more about your new world. And don't get discouraged! As Pope St. John Paul II said repeatedly, "Be not afraid." And remember St. Teresa of Calcutta's profound words that serve as a proper perspective: "Christ doesn't call me to be successful, He calls me to be faithful."

Wendy: See you later, Dad. Love you.

Joe: You, too, hon. Give me a little time to get acclimated and let's make a plan. Despite the mess that may surround us, let's also remember the Catholic organization *The Christophers'* motto: "Better to light one candle than to curse the darkness." God bless!

www.ingramcontent.com/pod-product-compliance
Lightning Source LLC
Chambersburg PA
CBHW070808280326
41934CB00012B/3103